First World War
and Army of Occupation
War Diary
France, Belgium and Germany

27 DIVISION
Divisional Troops
A Squadron Surrey Yeomanry
21 December 1914 - 28 October 1915

WO95/2257/1

The Naval & Military Press Ltd
www.nmarchive.com
Published in association with The National Archives

Published by

The Naval & Military Press Ltd

Unit 10 Ridgewood Industrial Park,

Uckfield, East Sussex,

TN22 5QE England

Tel: +44 (0) 1825 749494

www.naval-military-press.com

www.nmarchive.com

This diary has been reprinted in facsimile from the original. Any imperfections are inevitably reproduced and the quality may fall short of modern type and cartographic standards.

© **Crown Copyright**
Images reproduced by permission of The National Archives, London, England, 2015.

Contents

Document type	Place/Title	Date From	Date To
Heading	WO95/2257/1		
Heading	27th Division Divl Troops 'A' Sqn Surrey Yeo. Dec 1914-Oct 1915		
Heading	A Squadron Friday Yeo (Divl Cov 27th Div) Vol I 21.12.14-27.2.15 Oct 15		
War Diary	Winchester	21/12/1914	31/12/1914
War Diary	Wallon Cappel	31/12/1914	05/01/1915
War Diary	Boeschepe	06/01/1915	27/02/1915
Heading	A. Squadn Furrey Yeo. (27th Divl Cavalry) Vol II 1-31.3.15		
War Diary		01/03/1915	31/03/1915
War Diary		13/03/1915	22/03/1915
Heading	27th Division "A" Squadn Furrey Yeo. (27th Divl. Cavy.) Vol III 1.4.-31.5.15		
War Diary	Boescheppe	01/04/1915	30/04/1915
War Diary		24/04/1915	29/04/1915
War Diary		01/05/1915	31/05/1915
Heading	27th Division "A" Squadn Furrey Yeo. (27th Divl Cavy) Vol IV From 4th June To 27th July 1915		
War Diary	Croix De Bac	04/06/1915	30/06/1915
War Diary		24/06/1915	24/06/1915
War Diary	Croix De Bac	02/07/1915	27/07/1915
War Diary	27th Division "A" Sqn Surrey Yeo. Aug-Oct Vol V		
War Diary	Croix De Bac	01/08/1915	16/09/1915
War Diary	Croix De Bac	03/09/1915	23/10/1915
War Diary	Mericourt	23/10/1915	31/10/1915
War Diary	Coignemicourt	28/10/1915	28/10/1915

WO95/2257/1

27TH DIVISION
DIVL TROOPS

'A' SQN SURREY YEO.
DEC 1914 - OCT 1915

To Salonika

$\frac{121}{4586}$

A. Squadron. Surrey Yeo: (Div¹ Cav: 27ᵗʰ Divⁿ).

Vol I 21.12.14 — 27.2.15

Oct '15

WAR DIARY or INTELLIGENCE SUMMARY

(Erase heading not required.)

Army Form C. 2118.

Hour, Date, Place	Summary of Events and Information	Remarks and references to Appendices
WINCHESTER Dec 21st 1914	Squadron left MAGDALEN HILL CAMP at 9.30 a.m. 6 Officers, 134 other ranks, 2 A.S.C. (attached) 160 horses. Embarked SOUTHAMPTON S.S. Architect, all on board by 4.30 pm. Left docks 8 pm.	
Dec 22nd	Reach HAVRE early after good crossing. Disembarked at mid-day Spent night in goods shed.	
Dec 23rd	Train left HAVRE 12.55 pm	
Dec 24th	Train arrived ARQUES 10am after good journey. Detraining very slow owing to lack of sufficient ramps. Marched to billets near WALLON CAPPEL in 10 farms, all men & horses under cover.	
Dec 25th – Dec 31st WALLON CAPPEL	Horses suffered considerably with cracked heels & mud fever, the result of MAGDALEN HILL CAMP and OLD PARK FARM, CANTERBURY	

C. A. Calvert Major
A Squadron

WAR DIARY or INTELLIGENCE SUMMARY

Army Form C. 2118.

Hour, Date, Place	Summary of Events and Information	Remarks and references to Appendices
WALLON CAPPEL Jan 1st – Jan 5th 1915	Had one long reconnaissance day through FORET DE NIEPPE, otherwise gave men + horses an easy time.	
Jan 6th BOECHEPE	Marched at 9.30 am. to BOECHEPE, Billeted in 4 farms, all horses under cover.	
Jan 7th	Made reports on roads in Divisional area. Duties. Traffic control – searching farms for stragglers – acting as guides to Infantry detachments – conducting drafts from Station – fetching remounts from railhead – patrolling telegraph + telephone wires – finding orderlies – carrying dispatches	
Jan 16th	The 2nd Troop under Lt. E. Bell left to join the Vth Army Corps Head Quarters at HAZEBROUCK.	
Jan 31st	Kept the roads for the 28 Division who marched through the 27th area	

C. A. Calvert Major
O.C. A' Squadron Surrey Yeo.

WAR DIARY or INTELLIGENCE SUMMARY

Army Form C. 2118.

Hour, Date, Place	Summary of Events and Information	Remarks and references to Appendices
BOESCHEPE Feb 1st & 2nd 1915	Kept the roads for the 28th Division who marched through the 2nd area.	
Feb 2nd 4 pm	Turned out & ordered to march at once to RENINGHELST, night alarm from the 28th Division. Tied horses up in field, men in huts.	
Feb 3rd	2nd Troop returned from Vth Corps.	
" 4th	Returned to billets but remained standing to.	
	Still standing to.	
Feb 14th	Turned out at 4.15 pm, marched to WESTOUTRE where remained in a farm. 28th Division attacked.	
" 15th – 16th	Remained in farm at WESTOUTRE.	
" 17th	Returned to BOESCHEPE midday, turned out again at 1 pm, went to RENINGHELST, horses in field, men in huts.	
" 18th	Returned to BOESCHEPE.	
" 22nd	Horses inspected by D.D.R. who was very complimentary on appearance.	
" 23rd	Sent Subalterns & sergeants to see Divisional Cavalry work done by XVth Hussars under Capt. Courage who kindly gave us much useful instruction.	
" 24th	Special road reports on all roads from BERTHEN to ST. SYLVESTRE CAPPEL.	

C.A. Calvert Major
O.C. "A" Squadron

121/4940.

A. Squadn Surrey Yeo:
(27th Divl Cavalry)

Vol II 1- 31. 3. 15.

WAR DIARY or INTELLIGENCE SUMMARY

Army Form C. 2118.

Hour, Date, Place	Summary of Events and Information	Remarks and references to Appendices
March 1st – 31st	The Squadron was employed in the usual duties i.e. Road patrols, orderly work, marching drafts from Railhead to units, meeting & delivering remounts. A small range was made and the whole squadron practised in ~~rifle~~ musketry. Troop leaders constantly had their troops out on reconnaissance work (practice).	
March 13th – 18th	Lt. E. Bell, Cpl. Holloway, Ptes. Crookenden & Fiss were attached to the 81st Bde at DICKEBUSCH to stalk snipers. When there the attack on St. ELOI took place.	
March 21st	Draft of 16 men arrived from England.	
March 22nd	Inspected billeting area in & behind YPRES.	

C. A. Calverthorp
O.C. "A" Squadron Surrey (D.L.R.) Yeomanry
27th Divn.

27th Division

121/55/4

"A" Squad Surrey Yeo.
(27th Divl: Cavy:)

Vol III   1.4 — 31.5.15.

WAR DIARY ~~or INTELLIGENCE SUMMARY~~

Army Form C. 2118.

(Erase heading not required.)

Hour, Date, Place	Summary of Events and Information	Remarks and references to Appendices
April 1st – 4th BOESCHEPPE	Usual orderly work, road control and a draft to CANADA NUTS.	
4th	After church parade marched to new quarters W of VLAMERTINGHE.	
5th & 6th	Visited new area for billets for Division. Squadron billeted in POPPERINGHE.	
7th	Moved to a new billett in a farm near BUSSEBOOM.	
8th	Cleaned up farm and built shelters.	
10th	Lt. H Bell & 2 men went to 80th Bde to look for snipers. Major Cockart President of a D.C.M.	
19th	Head Quarters moved from YPRES to POTIEZE.	
4th – 18th	Usual routine orderly work, meeting & conducting drafts, meeting and distributing remounts, inspecting & reporting on billeting accommodation in the Divisional area.	
19th	YPRES heavily shelled.	

# WAR DIARY or INTELLIGENCE SUMMARY

(Erase heading not required.)

Army Form C. 2118.

Hour, Date, Place	Summary of Events and Information	Remarks and references to Appendices
23rd – 30th	Collected the rations of the Division, R E stores and S.A.A and sent them off down the road at times where & when the shelling least severe. Also any drafts of men returning from hospital.	
24th	Cavalry Corps arrived up. Our billet used as Corps refracting centre also a Brigade camped in field.	
27th	VLAMERTINGHE shelled.	
28th	Pte Barker wounded in arm.	
29th	A large draft of 194 horses fetched from HAZEBROUCK.	

P. A. Calvert Major
O.C. A Squadron Divy ho
Div ho
27th Div.

WAR DIARY
or
INTELLIGENCE SUMMARY
(Erase heading not required.)

Army Form C. 2118.

Instructions regarding War Diaries and Intelligence Summaries are contained in F. S. Regs., Part II. and the Staff Manual respectively. Title pages will be prepared in manuscript.

Hour, Date, Place	Summary of Events and Information	Remarks and references to Appendices
May. 1st — 4th	Lt E Ball & 2nd Lt F Phillips with 60 men made a day out for C.O.C at advanced H.Q.	
3rd	2nd Lt Bruce & party buried horses in YPRES. Cpt Barclay fetched mules from HAZEBROUCK	
6th — 19th	1st E Bell and 2nd troop went to Adv. H.Qs as guard to C.O.C.	
4th	Lt H. Bell reconnoitred roads for rations S. of YPRES.	
9th	2nd Lt Bruce. draft at POPPERINGHE.	
	Captain Barclay & 2nd Lt Bruce fetched a large consignment of ~~remounts~~ recruits from GODDESWAERSVELDE remained there all night	
	2nd H. Bell met draft at POPPERINGHE	
14th — 19th	Squadron moved into dug outs W of YPRES	
1st — 19th	Sent ration parties off every night to different battalions, electing roads etc.	
19th	Moved into new billet between BOESCHEPPE & POPPERINGHE.	
~~18th~~	Went with Captain Barclay & party of men with wagons & cleared the Stores out of Ordnance Stores in ~~YPRES~~ YPRES.	

WAR DIARY ~~or INTELLIGENCE SUMMARY~~

Army Form C. 2118.

(Erase heading not required.)

Hour, Date, Place	Summary of Events and Information	Remarks and references to Appendices
20th	Went with 2nd Lt Brace & party with wagons and cleared out stores from the Infantry barracks.	
21st	Met a large draft at POPPERINGHE	
22nd	Capt Barclay & 2nd Lt Brace & party met 144 horses at GODDESWAERSVELDE. Went with A.P.M. & 30 busses to meet 82nd Bde coming out of trenches. Left 10.30 p.m. got back 7 a.m. 2nd Lt E Bell met draft at POPPERINGHE.	
24th	Squadron moved into bivouacs in a field near the C.O.'s farm. 1st Lt E Bell reconnoitred & marked the G.H.Q 2nd line for C.O. Germans attacked trenches with gas 28th Div driven back.	
25th	Met draft at POPPERINGHE	
26th	Capt Barclay & A P M met 81st Bde with busses coming out of trenches. Took 8 busses to pick up stragglers of 82nd Bde to LOCRE.	
27th	Met draft at POPPERINGHE	
28th		

WAR DIARY or INTELLIGENCE SUMMARY

Army Form C. 2118.

Hour, Date, Place	Summary of Events and Information	Remarks and references to Appendices
May 29th	Captain Barclay and draft at POPPERINGHE.	
30th	Marched at 7 a.m. to new billets at CROIX de BAC relieving the VI Div. We took over quarters occupied by Northamptonshire from army. Found Guard of 1 N.C.O and 12 men for bridge over R. LYS.	
31st	Usual orderly work and routine carried out during month. 4 horses killed and a few wounded.	

C. A. Calvert Major
O.C. "A" Squadron hurry ho
Div. ho
27th Div.

27th Division

121/6427

"A Squad" Surrey Yeo. (27th Div Cavy)

Vol IV

From 4th June to 27th July 1915.

WAR DIARY or INTELLIGENCE SUMMARY

Army Form C. 2118.

Hour, Date, Place	Summary of Events and Information	Remarks and references to Appendices
CROIX de BAC June	Had to learn new district. Find guard 2 N.C.Os and 10 men on BAC St MAUR bridge. Four N.C.Os & men on leave each week towards the end of month. Squadron drill on River bank	
4th	Draft of 7 men arrived for Squadron met by Lt. Phillips.	
6th	Lt H Bell met remounts 6 for Squadron	
7th	Found billets for R.F.A.	
9th — 14th	Leave to England Major Calvert	
17th	Major Calvert president of F.G.C.M.	
19th — 25th	Captain Barclay leave to England	
21st	Lt H Bell met remounts	
22nd — 30th	Major Calvert acted A.P.M. for Division	

Hour, Date, Place	Summary of Events and Information	Remarks and references to Appendices
22nd	Major Calvert, Lt. H.J. Bell, Sergeant Shields and Pte. Barley mentioned in Sir J. French's despatches	
24th	Major Calvert received D.S.O.	
30th	Major Calvert returned to Squadron.	
24th	2nd Lt. J. Phillips went to POPPERINGHE to meet H.D. Jones.	

C. A. Calverthuysen
O.C. Div: ps
27th Div.

WAR DIARY or INTELLIGENCE SUMMARY

Army Form C. 2118.

Hour, Date, Place	Summary of Events and Information	Remarks and references to Appendices
July CROIX de BAC	Usual work and exercise. The Squadron supplied a party daily for digging and putting up barbed wire entanglements in the subsidiary line. N.C.O's & men went on leave every week.	
2nd	2nd Lt. A.F. Drewe met draft.	
3rd	2nd Lt. J. Phillips met draft	
5th	Lt H Bell met reinforcements	
7th	Lt H Bell met draft	
9th — 15th	Lt H Bell leave to England	
13th — 20th	Lt E Bell leave to England	
14th	Major Cabnet member of General Court-Martial.	
15th	Major Cabnet went billeting in morning, in afternoon went round subsidiary line to inspect wire entanglement positions with Adj. R.E.	
22nd — 29th	2nd Lt J. Phillips on leave to England	

WAR DIARY or INTELLIGENCE SUMMARY

Army Form C. 2118.

Hour, Date, Place	Summary of Events and Information	Remarks and references to Appendices
21st	Captain Barclay met draft	
22nd	Lt H. Bell went billeting	
26th	Major Cabnet & Capt. Barclay President & member of a Court of Inquiry at bombing school	
26th	2nd Lt A. F. Druce went on leave to England	
27th	Lts H & E Bell went out billeting.	

Captain Barclay made claims officer of the Division at beginning of month.

C. A. Cabnet Major
O.C. Div. Pro
27th Div

27th Division

"A" Sqn Surrey Yeo.

Aug - Oct

Vol V

121/7551

WAR DIARY
or
INTELLIGENCE SUMMARY
(Erase heading not required.)

Army Form C. 2118.

Instructions regarding War Diaries and Intelligence Summaries are contained in F.S. Regs., Part II. and the Staff Manual respectively. Title pages will be prepared in manuscript.

Hour, Date, Place	Summary of Events and Information	Remarks and references to Appendices
Croix de Bac CROIX de BAC August 1st — 4th	Work on subsidiary line putting up barbed wire entanglements. Usual duties by officers — meeting drafts — repairing on roads — billeting etc.	
	Had parties of men out continually helping farmers in the neighbourhood with their harvest	
5th — 11th	Party of Officers & men of the Westmorland & Cumberland Yeomanry attached for instruction	
12th — 17th	A new party of 6 Officers & 90 men Westmorland & Cumberland Yeomanry attached for instruction	
24th	Squadron inspected by G.O.C. Division	

WAR DIARY or INTELLIGENCE SUMMARY

Army Form C. 2118.

Hour, Date, Place	Summary of Events and Information	Remarks and references to Appendices
August 25th — 30th	O.C. with 1st & 3rd troops (3/# 59 O.R) went into the trenches attached to the P.P.C.L.I. C. A. Calvert Major O.C. "A" Squadron Surrey Yeomanry Div. Jo. 27th Div.	

WAR DIARY or INTELLIGENCE SUMMARY

Army Form C. 2118.

Hour, Date, Place	Summary of Events and Information	Remarks and references to Appendices
September 1st — 16th CROIX DE BAC	Usual duties	
3rd — 8th	Captain Barclay with 2nd & 4th Troops went into the trenches and were attached to the D.C.L.I.	
16th	Squadron marched to MERRIS.	
19th	Marched to and entrained at THIENNES.	
20th	Detrained at LONGEAU & marched to MERICOURT. Bivouacked	
26th	Moved into billets	

P. A. Calvert Major
O.C. A Squadron Surrey Yeomanry
Div. to 27th Division

WAR DIARY or **INTELLIGENCE SUMMARY**

Army Form C. 2118.

Hour, Date, Place	Summary of Events and Information	Remarks and references to Appendices
October 1st — 23rd MERICOURT	Continued work on 2nd line putting up barbed wire entanglements. O.C. Squadron was put in charge of all wiring parties on this line. Found posts and patrols for control of civilian traffic also a post on canal between divisions at Mericourt. Usual duties such as pitching lines, billeting etc.	
23rd	Marched to PONT de METZ billeted there one night.	
24th	Marched to GUIGNEMICOURT.	
24th — 31st GUIGNEMICOURT	Only duty finding 1 post on road. Meeting & remounts at AILLY.	
28th	Pte E.H. Pellowe died of heart failure.	

P.A. Calvert Major
O.C. A Squadron Surrey Yeomanry
Div. for 27th Div.

www.ingramcontent.com/pod-product-compliance
Lightning Source LLC
Chambersburg PA
CBHW081250170426
43191CB00037B/2110